D1015838

A GIFT FOR:

_____

FROM:

_____

ANDY GRIFFITH

BOUND *for the* PROMISED LAND

Nashville, Tennessee

Introduction

We're all going somewhere. Some are going up the mountain; others are going down into the valley. Even when we think we're standing still, the earth itself is moving and taking us with it.

Without help, we're bound to wander and get lost out here, so we turn to the only beacon in all of time—a rugged Cross on a lonely hill. From that rough pedestal, Jesus directs us heavenward, and just to make sure the journey is as clear as possible, He sends His Spirit to guide us to the Promised Land.

So many of our most beloved hymns celebrate this journey, giving us musical pictures of where we've been while motivating us to keep going. Like a scrapbook, *Bound for the Promised Land* is a collection of many of my favorite snapshots along the way. I hope these thoughts inspire you as they've inspired me so many times, and I'm looking forward to seeing you on the other side of the river.

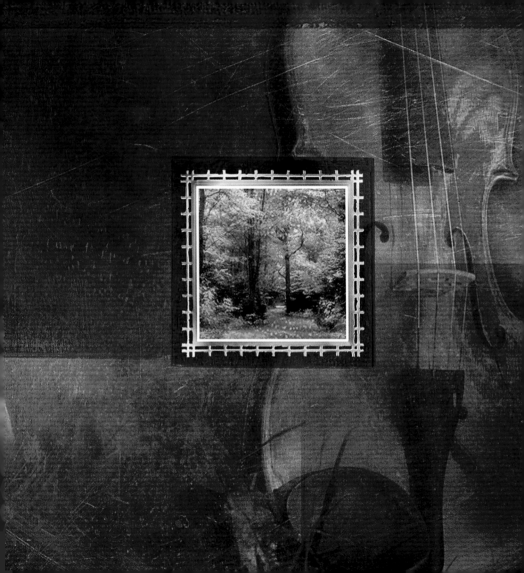

Setting Forth

Every journey has to begin somewhere. For many of us that journey begins in a good home with family, friends, a church, and many more blessings. Others start out with much less. But whether we have a little or a lot, we're still starting the trip to the Promised Land in the middle of nowhere. We're simply lost. So we turn toward the Cross where Jesus waits to point us in the right direction for the road ahead.

Here are some of my favorite hymns about finding the Cross and starting the journey.

Just As I Am
Jesus, I Come
Down at the Cross
Take the Name of Jesus with You
What Wondrous Love is This?
Jesus, Lover of My Soul

The Old Rugged Cross
Softly and Tenderly
I Surrender All
Grace Greater Than Our Sin
What a Friend We Have in Jesus
Near the Cross

SINGING FROM THE START

Mama played guitar a little and sang
at home, but one of the earliest times that
I remember singing hymns was in Sunday
school. I was a little boy, I don't remember
how old, but we were singing "Jesus Loves
Me" and everybody would look at me, I guess
because I was singing so loud. Either that
or I was off-tune, I don't know. But that's
my very earliest memory of singing.

Jesus Loves Me
Anna B. Warner, 1860

Jesus loves me! This I know,
For the Bible tells me so.
Little ones to Him belong;
They are weak, but He is strong.

Yes, Jesus loves me!
Yes, Jesus loves me!
Yes, Jesus loves me!
The Bible tells me so.

CONNECTING TO GOD
& EACH OTHER

One of the reasons people love hymns so much is that they connect us to the past and connect us to each other here in the present. They are a beautiful tradition that so many of us share.

In my formative years I sang all around town. The very first solo I ever sang was in the Second Baptist Church in Mt. Airy, North Carolina. I sang "Sweet Hour of Prayer." I was 14, probably. In other churches, I sang songs like "Open the Gates of the Temple," "Prayer Perfect," "Sing Hallelujah, Praise the Lord," and others that I'd learned in the Moravian church. And I sang an Easter cantata at the Presbyterian church once.

What all the songs and all the churches had in common was Jesus.

Sweet Hour of Prayer

W. W. Walford, 1845

Sweet hour of prayer, sweet hour of prayer!
That calls me from a world of care,
And bids me at my Father's throne,
Make all my wants and wishes known.
In seasons of distress and grief
My soul has often found relief,
And oft escaped the tempter's snare
By thy return, sweet hour of prayer.

Sweet hour of prayer, sweet hour of prayer!
Thy wings shall my petition bear
To Him whose truth and faithfulness
Engage the waiting soul to bless.
And since He bids me seek His face,
Believe His Word, and trust His grace,
I'll cast on Him my ev'ry care,
And wait for thee, sweet hour of prayer.

"Sweet Prospect" is a very old hymn that still moves me.

It has been so much a favorite of mine

that we had a choir to sing it on a *Matlock* show.

Sweet Prospect

Also known as 'Bound for the Promised Land'
or 'On Jordan's Stormy Banks I Stand'

Samuel Stennett, 1787

On Jordan's stormy banks I stand,
And cast a wishful eye,
To Canaan's fair and happy land,
Where my possessions lie.

O'er all those wide extended plains,
Shines one eternal day;
There God the Son forever reigns,
And scatters night away.

I am bound for the Promised Land
I am bound for the Promised Land
Oh, who will come and go with me?
I am bound for the Promised Land

Oh, the transporting, rapt'rous
  scene,
That rises to my sight,
Sweet fields arrayed in living
  green,
And rivers of delight.

No chilling winds, or pois'nous
  breath,
Can reach that healthful shore;
Sickness and sorrow, pain and
  death
Are felt and feared no more.

Shape-Note Singing

I learned "Sweet Prospect" out of the *Sacred Harp Hymnal*. Those hymnals were shape-notes, and people learned to sing by solfege—Do-Re-Mi-Fa-So-La-Ti-Do. They would first sing the hymn through with solfege. Then they would sing it through with the words.

I made a mistake on "Sweet Prospect" when I learned the top line, which is a part; the melody is in the tenor. Later, we were doing a movie with Johnny Cash, and I wanted Johnny to sing that hymn on one of his records. I went in there and sang it for him, and he said, "Are you singing a part?" And I said, "No, that's the tune." And he called out, "Andy can read music! June, Andy can read music!"

SWEET PROSPECT.

On Jor - dan's stormy banks I stand, And cast a wish-ful...
To Ca - naan's fair and hap-py land, Where my pos - ses - sions...

... to my sight, Sweet fields ar-...

'We Must've Gone to the Same Church'

I remember when we were choosing hymns for the record. We were in the office of Billy Ray Hearn, from Sparrow Records, the very first time I ever met him, and we had a hymn book out. I told the piano player in there, "Drop everything a third," because the way it was written was too high for me. Then Billy Ray and I, we kept singing and singing and singing and singing, and Billy Ray said, "We must've gone to the same church!"

I knew every hymn that he knew.

The Old Rugged Cross

George Bennard, 1913

On a hill far away stood an old rugged cross,
The emblem of suffering and shame;
And I love that old cross where the dearest and best
For a world of lost sinners was slain.

So I'll cherish the old rugged cross,
Till my trophies at last I lay down;
I will cling to the old rugged cross,
And exchange it some day for a crown.

To the old rugged cross I will ever be true;
Its shame and reproach gladly bear;
Then He'll call me some day to my home far away,
Where His glory forever I'll share.

Sharing the Music

Music often figured into my television shows, both on-camera and off-camera.

When they would light Don Knotts and me for scenes in the *Andy Griffith Show*, Don and I would often sing hymns in harmony. Don has a beautiful tenor. Once on the *Andy Griffith Show*, we did an episode called "Man in a Hurry." I had my guitar, and Don and I sang "Church in the Wildwood," and the man who was in a hurry sang along with us.

Often on *Matlock* when Matlock would be in the kitchen cooking or something, he would hum a hymn. I also did a show on *Matlock* called "The Blues Singer," and I sang "Just a Closer Walk with Thee" with a friend of mine, the blues singer Brownie McGhee. I've known that song a long time, but I learned Brownie's way of doing it.

I am weak, but Thou art strong;
Jesus, keep me from all wrong;
I'll be satisfied as long
As I walk, let me walk close to Thee.

Just a closer walk with Thee,
Grant it, Jesus, is my plea,
Daily walking close to Thee,
Let it be, dear Lord, let it be.

Through this world of toil and snares,
If I falter, Lord, who cares?
Who with me my burden shares?
None but Thee, dear Lord, none but Thee.

When my feeble life is o'er,
Time for me will be no more;
Guide me gently, safely o'er
To Thy kingdom shore, to Thy shore.

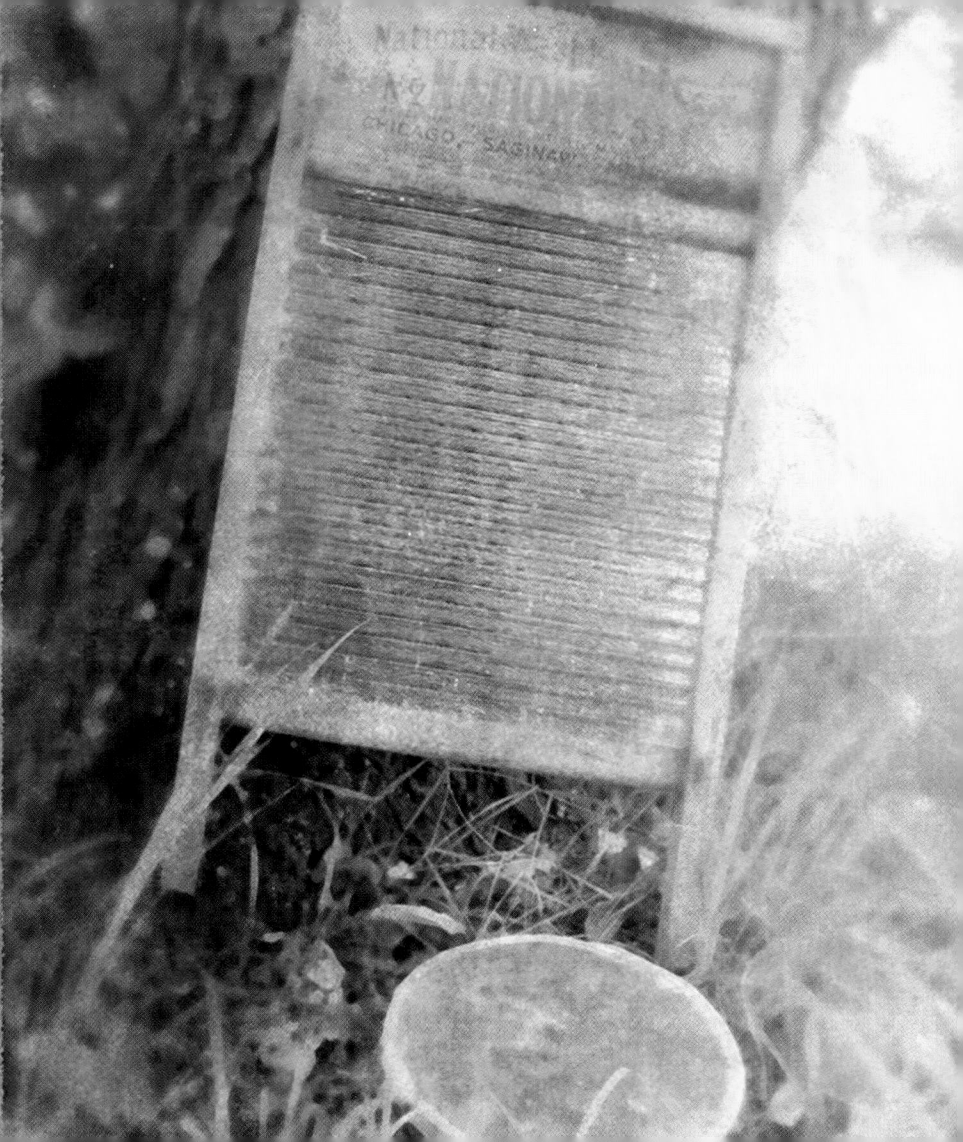
CHICAGO, SAGINAW

Church in the Wildwood

William S. Pitts, 1857

There's a church in the valley by the wildwood
No lovelier spot in the dale
No place is so dear to my childhood
As the little brown church in the vale

(Oh, come, come, come, come)

Come to the church by the wildwood
Oh, come to the church in the vale
No spot is so dear to my childhood
As the little brown church in the vale

How sweet on a clear Sabbath morning
To listen to the clear ringing bells
Its tones so sweetly are calling
Oh come to the church in the vale

As the Israelites journeyed to the Promised Land,
they celebrated in song the One who made the promise possible.

❧

Then Moses and the children of Israel

sang this song to the LORD, and spoke, saying:

"I will sing to the LORD,

For He has triumphed gloriously!

The horse and its rider

He has thrown into the sea!

The LORD is my strength and song,

And He has become my salvation;

He is my God, and I will praise Him;

My father's God, and I will exalt Him.

—EXODUS 15:1, 2

DOWN AT THE CROSS

Elisha A. Hoffman, 1878

Down at the cross where my Savior died,
Down where for cleansing from sin I cried,
There to my heart was the blood applied;
Glory to His Name!

Glory to His Name, glory to His Name:
There to my heart was the blood applied;
Glory to His Name!

I am so wondrously saved from sin,
Jesus so sweetly abides within;
There at the cross where He took me in;
Glory to His Name!

Come to this fountain so rich and sweet,
Cast thy poor soul at the Savior's feet;
Plunge in today, and be made complete;
Glory to His Name!

Take the Name
of Jesus With You

Lydia O. Baxter, 1870

Take the Name of Jesus with you,
Child of sorrow and of woe,
It will joy and comfort give you;
Take it then, where'er you go.

How it thrills our souls with joy,
When His loving arms receive us,
And His songs our tongues
    employ!

Precious Name, O how sweet!
Hope of earth and joy of Heav'n.
Precious Name, O how sweet!
Hope of earth and joy of Heav'n.

Take the Name of Jesus ever,
As a shield from every snare;
If temptations round you gather,
Breathe that holy Name in prayer.
O the precious Name of Jesus!

At the Name of Jesus bowing,
Falling prostrate at His feet,
King of kings in heav'n we'll
    crown Him,
When our journey is complete.

For the land which you go to possess

is not like the land of Egypt

from which you have come,

where you sowed your seed and

watered it by foot, as a vegetable garden;

but the land which you cross over

to possess is a land of hills and valleys,

which drinks water from the rain of heaven,

a land for which the LORD your God cares;

the eyes of the LORD your God

are always on it, from the beginning

of the year to the very end of the year.

—DEUTERONOMY 11:10-12

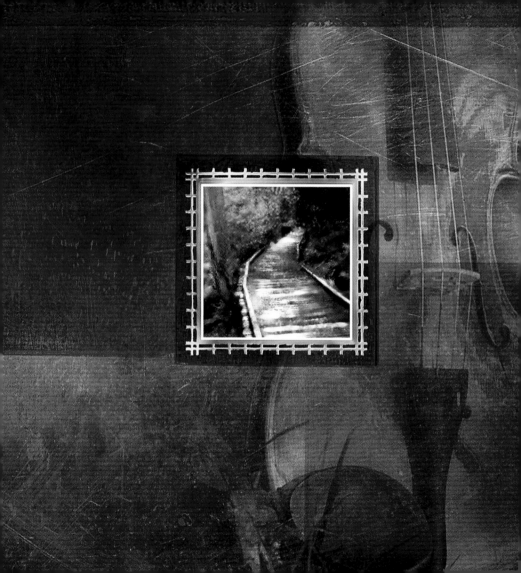

Along the Way

Sometimes the journey to the Promised Land is easy; other times it's tough. The point is to keep going, no matter what.

Hymns are some of our best companions for the journey. They remind us that we're travelers with a purpose, and they comfort us when we're tired. We have hope along our earthly paths, because we have a heavenly destination. Hymns are our walking tunes, our marching cadences, our campfire reveries.

Some of my favorite hymns along the way are:

Jesus, Savior, Pilot Me
I Need Thee Every Hour
All the Way My Savior Leads Me
Leaning on the Everlasting Arms
Does Jesus Care?
His Eye is on the Sparrow
God Will Take Care of You
'Tis So Sweet to Trust in Jesus
Take Time to be Holy

Onward, Christian Soldiers
We're Marching to Zion
Stand Up, Stand Up for Jesus
Go, Tell It on the Mountain
I Wonder as I Wander
Jesus Walked This Lonesome Valley
Sweet Hour of Prayer
Whispering Hope

Hymns Point to Jesus

The music is changing in many worship services. Some people are seeking more contemporary or pop music worship, and some are seeking more traditional music. In our church, we have an 8:30 service and an 11 o'clock service. The 8:30 service is where they're doing the more contemporary music, and Cindi and I go to the 11 o'clock for traditional music. I'm more comfortable with that.

Most of the contemporary songs don't really catch me, but a hymn is a hymn, as long as it's moving somebody toward Jesus, if it's worshipping Jesus and the values that He taught us. Some regular songs can do that. For instance, "Bridge Over Troubled Water," sung by Simon and Garfunkel, has some of the concepts of great hymns, even though it isn't a hymn.

Jesus, Savior, Pilot Me

(The Sailor's Hymn) *Edward Hopper, 1871*

Jesus, Savior, pilot me
Over life's tempestuous sea;
Unknown waves before me roll,
Hiding rock and treacherous shoal.
Chart and compass come from Thee;
Jesus, Savior, pilot me.

As a mother stills her child,
Thou canst hush the ocean wild;
Boisterous waves obey Thy will,
When Thou sayest to them, "Be still!"
Wondrous Sovereign of the sea,
Jesus, Savior, pilot me.

When at last I near the shore,
And the fearful breakers roar
'Twixt me and the peaceful rest,
Then, while leaning on Thy breast,
May I hear Thee say to me,
"Fear not, I will pilot thee."

Just As I Am

～

I've never written a hymn or a song.
I don't have that talent. God only gave
me two-and-a-half talents. I'm an
actor—and a pretty good actor—and I
can sing, and I can write a little.
That's the half talent.

The point is to use what
God gave you, just as
you are.

Just As I Am
Charlotte Elliot, 1835

Just as I am, without one plea,
But that Thy blood was shed for me,
And that Thou bidst me come to Thee,
O Lamb of God, I come, I come.

Just as I am, though tossed about
With many a conflict, many a doubt,
Fightings and fears within, without,
O Lamb of God, I come, I come.

Just as I am, Thou wilt receive,
Wilt welcome, pardon, cleanse, relieve;
Because Thy promise I believe,
O Lamb of God, I come, I come.

Just as I am, of that free love
The breadth, length, depth, and height to prove,
Here for a season, then above,
O Lamb of God, I come, I come!

Timeless Sentiment

What makes a hymn timeless is the sentiment in it. "It Is Well With My Soul" is one of those timeless songs.

In the last year of *Matlock*, we had an actress on the show named Carol Houston, and she was a wonderful singer. We arranged for her to sing "It Is Well With My Soul" with this great Congregational Christian choir, and boy was it powerful.

Those who wait on the LORD
Shall renew their strength;
They shall mount up with wings like eagles,
They shall run and not be weary,
They shall walk and not faint.

—Isaiah 40:31

It Is Well With My Soul

Horatio G. Spafford, 1873

When peace like a river attendeth my way,
When sorrows like sea billows roll,
Whatever my lot Thou hast taught me to say,
"It is well, it is well with my soul."

It is well with my soul.
It is well with my soul.
It is well, it is well with my soul.

My sin, oh the bliss of this glorious thought,
My sin, not in part, but the whole
Is nailed to the cross and I bear it no more.
Praise the Lord, praise the Lord, O my soul.

And Lord, haste the day when the faith shall be sight,
The clouds be rolled back as a scroll.
The trump shall resound, and the Lord shall descend,
Even so, it is well with my soul.

A Lullaby for Jesus

I did a Christmas album called *The Christmas Guest* in 2003.
One of my favorite songs on the album was "Away in a
Manger." I love singing "Away in a Manger," even though it
seems strange for a man to sing it. I loved it, and I still love it.

It's a another timeless song. Children sing it. 78-year-old men
sing it. It's moving for us all.

I will pray with the spirit,
and I will also pray with the understanding.
I will sing with the spirit,
and I will also sing with the understanding.

—1 Corinthians 14:15

Away in a Manger

Verses 1 & 2, anonymous, 1885
Verse 3, John T. McFarland, before 1913

Away in a manger, no crib for a bed,
The little Lord Jesus laid down His sweet head.
The stars in the sky looked down where He lay,
The little Lord Jesus, asleep on the hay.

The cattle are lowing, the Baby awakes,
But little Lord Jesus, no crying He makes;
I love Thee, Lord Jesus, look down from the sky
And stay by my cradle til morning is nigh.

Be near me, Lord Jesus, I ask Thee to stay
Close by me forever, and love me, I pray;
Bless all the dear children in Thy tender care,
And fit us for heaven to live with Thee there.

On the end of "*Away in a Manger*," I went into
"*Golden Slumber Kiss Your Eyes*," which is a beautiful song.
It was almost like singing a lullaby to Jesus.

GOLDEN SLUMBER
Thomas Dekker, 1603

Golden slumber kiss your eyes
Smiles await you when you rise.
Sleep pretty baby, don't you cry
And I will sing you lullaby.

You will bring them in and plant them

In the mountain of Your inheritance,

In the place, O LORD, which You have made

For Your own dwelling,

The sanctuary, O LORD,

which Your hands have established.

—Exodus 15:17

At midnight Paul and Silas

were praying and singing hymns to God,

and the prisoners were listening to them.

—Acts 16:25

Comforting Our Souls

Hymns can be so comforting, like lullabies
for our souls, and I sometimes had my char-
acters show how much those songs mean.
One time, Matlock called a client by the
wrong name. He thought he was losing it
and was going to retire. As Matlock was
packing his things, he was sitting down
singing "Softly and Tenderly."

SOFTLY & TENDERLY
Will L. Thompson, 1880

Softly and tenderly Jesus is calling,
Calling for you and for me;
See, on the portals He's waiting and watching,
Watching for you and for me.

Come home, come home
Ye who are weary, come home.
Earnestly, tenderly Jesus is calling,
Calling oh sinner, come home.

Why should we tarry when Jesus is pleading,
Pleading for you and for me?
Why should we linger and heed not His mercies,
Mercies for you and for me?

Time is now fleeting, the moments are passing,
Passing from you and from me;
Shadows are gathering, death warnings coming,
Coming for you and for me.

I Need Thee Every Hour

Annie S. Hawks, 1872

I need Thee every hour, most gracious Lord;
No tender voice like Thine can peace afford.

I need Thee, O I need Thee;
Every hour I need Thee;
O bless me now, my Savior,
I come to Thee.

I need Thee every hour, stay Thou nearby;
Temptations lose their power when Thou art nigh.

I need Thee every hour, in joy or pain;
Come quickly and abide, or life is in vain.

I need Thee every hour; teach me Thy will;
And Thy rich promises in me fulfill.

I need Thee every hour, most Holy One;
O make me Thine indeed, Thou blessèd Son.

All the Way My Savior Leads Me

Fannie Crosby, 1875

All the way my Savior leads me
What have I to ask beside?
Can I doubt His tender mercy,
Who through life has been my Guide?
Heav'nly peace, divinest comfort,
Here by faith in Him to dwell!
For I know, whate'er befall me,
Jesus doeth all things well;
For I know, whate'er befall me,
Jesus doeth all things well.

All the way my Savior leads me
O the fullness of His love!
Perfect rest to me is promised
In my Father's house above.
When my spirit, clothed immortal,
Wings its flight to realms of day
This my song through endless ages:
Jesus led me all the way;
This my song through endless ages:
Jesus led me all the way.

A Long-Strumming Friendship

One constant throughout most of my career
has been my guitar. It's a Martin D-18 with a
clear pickguard. It was given to me to carry
around in one of my early movies, even though
I never played it in the film. The guitar had
been painted black, but in 1959 I took all the
paint off and had it refinished it to the natural
wood. I've played this guitar both on and off
my shows ever since, and every time you see a
guitar in this book, it's that same instrument
I've enjoyed for nearly 50 years.

Onward, Christian Soldiers

Sabine Baring-Gould, 1865

Onward, Christian soldiers, marching as to war,
With the cross of Jesus going on before.
Christ, the royal Master, leads against the foe;
Forward into battle see His banners go!

Onward, Christian soldiers, marching as to war,
With the cross of Jesus going on before.

Crowns and thrones may perish, kingdoms rise and wane,
But the church of Jesus constant will remain.
Gates of hell can never gainst that church prevail;
We have Christ's own promise, and that cannot fail.

Onward then, ye people, join our happy throng,
Blend with ours your voices in the triumph song.
Glory, laud and honor unto Christ the King,
This through countless ages men and angels sing.

Jesus, Lover of my Soul

Charles Wesley, 1740

Jesus, lover of my soul, let me to Thy bosom fly,
While the nearer waters roll, while the tempest still is high.
Hide me, O my Savior, hide, till the storm of life is past;
Safe into the haven guide; O receive my soul at last.

Other refuge have I none, hangs my helpless soul on Thee;
Leave, ah! leave me not alone, still support and comfort me.
All my trust on Thee is stayed, all my help from Thee I bring;
Cover my defenseless head with the shadow of Thy wing.

Thou, O Christ, art all I want, more than all in Thee I find;
Raise the fallen, cheer the faint, heal the sick, and lead the blind.
Just and holy is Thy Name, I am all unrighteousness;
False and full of sin I am; Thou art full of truth and grace.

Plenteous grace with Thee is found, grace to cover all my sin;
Let the healing streams abound; make and keep me pure within.
Thou of life the fountain art, freely let me take of Thee;
Spring Thou up within my heart; rise to all eternity.

TAKE TIME TO BE HOLY
William D. Longstaff, 1882

Take time to be holy, speak oft with thy Lord;
Abide in Him always, and feed on His Word.
Make friends of God's children, help those who are weak,
Forgetting in nothing His blessing to seek.

Take time to be holy, the world rushes on;
Spend much time in secret, with Jesus alone.
By looking to Jesus, like Him thou shalt be;
Thy friends in thy conduct His likeness shall see.

Take time to be holy, be calm in thy soul,
Each thought and each motive beneath His control.
Thus led by His Spirit to fountains of love,
Thou soon shalt be fitted for service above.

Joy for the Journey's End

Like the Israelites of old, we are bound for a Promised Land. It's a real place, with our real, happily-ever-after ending. Just thinking about the Promised Land makes our journey there so much sweeter. We can't sing enough about heaven on this side of the river, but when we finally arrive there, we'll be able to celebrate forever!

You will cross over the Jordan
and go in to possess the land
which the LORD your God is giving you,
and you will possess it and dwell in it.

—Deuteronomy 11:31

Inspired by 'Golden Bells'

One of my favorite songs is "When They Ring the Golden Bells." In many ways it's like a sermon in a song, because it says so much about our hope in Jesus and in the heaven He's preparing for us.

I love everything about the song. We don't know exactly how heaven is going to be, but I think that's a song that helps people have their own glimpses of what will happen when those golden bells ring and Jesus greets them. However it happens, that's such a beautiful thought to envision Jesus welcoming you into the new part of your life, the rest of your life. It's such a welcoming song.

When They Ring the Golden Bells

Daniel de Marbelle, 1887

There's a land beyond the river,
That we call the sweet forever,
And we only reach that shore by faith's decree;
One by one we'll gain the portals,
There to dwell with the immortals,
When they ring the golden bells for you and me.

Don't you hear the bells now ringing?
Don't you hear the angels singing?
'Tis the glory hallelujah Jubilee.
In that far off sweet forever,
Just beyond the shining river,
When they ring the golden bells for you and me.

When our days shall know their number,
And in death we sweetly slumber,
When the King commands the spirit to be free;
Nevermore with anguish laden,
We shall reach that lovely Eden,
When they ring the golden bells for you and me.

"When They Ring the Golden Bells" is how I got inspired to do albums of hymns. I did a record many years ago with Columbia, and the best cut on it was "When They Ring the Golden Bells for You and Me." When Steve Tyrell was down prerecording Randy Travis, I played it for him, and I told him I'd like to try recording hymns again sometime. Steve has a wonderful career now as a singer, but Steve at that time was mainly a producer and he helped make it happen.

We had the choir sing that in one *Matlock* show. Their choir director also played piano and organ, and during a rehearsal she played it the way it's written. BOP bop-BOP bop-BOP bop-BOP-BOP. Very staccato. And I said, "No, no, it's legato." I played my recording of it, so they could hear the smooth way to do it. Then we sang it on the show, and it was beautiful.

We, according to His promise,
look for new heavens and a new earth
in which righteousness dwells.
Therefore, beloved, looking forward
to these things, be diligent
to be found by Him in peace,
without spot and blameless;
and consider that the longsuffering
of our Lord is salvation.

— 2 Peter 3:13-15

JOY TO THE WORLD
Isaac Watts, 1719

Joy to the world, the Lord is come!
Let earth receive her King;
Let every heart prepare Him room,
And heaven and nature sing,
And heaven and nature sing,
And heaven, and heaven, and nature sing.

He rules the world with truth and grace,
And makes the nations prove
The glories of His righteousness,
And wonders of His love,
And wonders of His love,
And wonders, wonders, of His love.

The Unclouded Day

Josiah K. Alwood, 1880

O they tell me of a home far
    beyond the skies,
O they tell me of a home far
    away;
O they tell me of a home where
    no storm clouds rise,
O they tell me of an unclouded day.

O they tell me of a King in His
    beauty there,
And they tell me that mine eyes shall
    behold
Where He sits on the throne that is
    whiter than snow,
In the city that is made of gold.

O the land of cloudless day,
O the land of an unclouded day,
O they tell me of a home where no storm clouds rise,
O they tell me of an unclouded day.

O they tell me of a home where my
    friends have gone,
O they tell me of that land far away,
Where the tree of life in eternal
    bloom
Sheds its fragrance through the
    unclouded day.

O they tell me that He smiles on His
    children there,
And His smile drives their sorrows
    all away;
And they tell me that no tears ever
    come again
In that lovely land of unclouded day.

A New Name Written

C. Austin Miles, 1905

I was once a sinner, but I came
Pardon to receive from my Lord:
This was freely given, and
    I found
That He always kept His word.

There's a new name written down
    in glory,
And it's mine, O yes, it's mine!
And the white robed angels sing
    the story,
"A sinner has come home."
For there's a new name written
    down in glory,
And it's mine, O yes, it's mine!
With my sins forgiven I am bound
    for heaven,
Never more to roam.

I was humbly kneeling at the
    cross,
Fearing naught by God's angry
    frown;
When the heavens opened and
    I saw
That my name was written down.

In the Book 'tis written, "Saved
    by Grace,"
O the joy that came to my soul!
Now I am forgiven, and I know
By the blood I am made whole.

And they sang a new song, saying:

"You are worthy to take the scroll,

And to open its seals;

For You were slain,

And have redeemed us to God by Your blood

Out of every tribe and tongue and people and nation,

And have made us kings and priests to our God;

And we shall reign on the earth."

—REVELATION 5:9, 10

A Final Thought

I hope you've enjoyed this stroll through some
of my favorite hymns, and perhaps you've even
hummed along while you were reading. These
songs have encouraged and instructed people
for generations. Their truth is timeless, their
impact eternal.

Like these songs, may the music of your life
be heard all the way to the Promised Land.

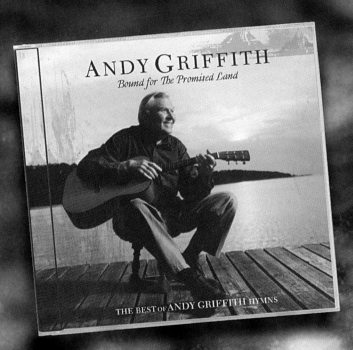